I0470943

Wealth Builders

Top 10 Reasons Why You Have Not Struck It Rich Yet!

Michael McCain

Wealth Builders: Michael McCain

indirectly, of the use and application of any of the contents of this book.

Maximize Publishing Inc.

2018 Monterey Ave

Bronx N.Y. 10457

Attn.: Michael McCain

C/o: Kevin Brown

ISBN-13:
978-1492241966

ISBN-10:
1492241962

Table Of Contents:

Wealth Builders: Michael McCain

Wealth Builders

Top Reasons Why You Have Not Struck It Rich Yet!

Wealth Builders: Michael McCain

Introduction

We live in a society and generation where people are driven towards building wealth. Some people's reason for the desire of wealth is the polar opposite of the extreme poverty that they have had to live in. In this case I believe that there's nothing wrong with this motive, yet the way that you go about it or the strategies used to build wealth are vitally important. I personally believe there will always be what we call "poor and rich". Depending the existing economy and what country that you live in the effects and chances of building substantial wealth and affluence can be a task. Not only a task but present factors that make your chances look impossible.

Wealth Builders: Michael McCain

American culture and living is prided on being the country of liberty, freedom and the pursuit of happiness. While these statements exist as a truth most people need to understand that every single American or non-American are afforded the same opportunities and when you're living in a foreign country your chances may vary depending the wealth and economic outlook of that country. Generally wealth can be attained by all, whether educated or not.

The most important goal for every person is building a strategy as to how they will build wealth. It's important that every person has a business plan for how they will grow success and wealth in their lives. It may sound crazy on the onset of things but it's the best way is to build a blueprint. A blueprint gives you all the details of things you need to work on to achieve your goals, a timeline for how long it takes to get there and a set goal for an amount or place you need to arrive to.

Chapter One:

Stop Acting Rich

I am sure no one will come off being as bold as I am to say right now that if you plan to be a wealth builder and obtain the status of living that is defined "affluent or wealthy", then you must immediately "Stop acting rich". All the behaviors that constitute "keeping up with the Jones'" must go out the window. In this book I have outline the top 10 reasons you have not struck it rich yet. This book is not intended to be very long but will be full of wisdom and power strategies for the people who know how to think and implement a plan to become a "wealth builder". Pull out your highlighter and highlight all the key steps and things that stand out to you that can help you improve your changes at building wealth.

Reason #1: You spend money like you're already rich.

In American society it is easy to fall subject to following behind the latest trends and high profiled celebrities for their status, influence and affluence in the world. The reality is many people want to be more like someone else rather than being the best authentic person that they are able to be being "themselves". Living authentically means you use everything your life, skill and education has afforded you to build wealth and live an outstanding life. You cannot always measure the standard of success by the way someone else lives their lives. People have to be careful of outside influences that they pattern their lives after that might not align with the purpose and destiny that is designed for their lives.

Wealth Builders: Michael McCain

Sure, it feels good to buy expensive
things, whether it's a luxury car,
designer clothes, a big house in the
burbs, or a tropical vacation. Even if you
don't necessarily buy pricey items, if you
consistently buy stuff you really don't
need, it still adds up fast. But the
shopping high only lasts until the guilt
and regret set in or the credit card bill
arrives or letters from the bank reporting
overdrafts. Most of us are guilty of living
beyond our means and using credit
cards more than we should. For those
of us making sufficient income every
month does not mean that our entire
check should be spent as it comes in. If
you have the ability to pay your bills and
still have a few hundred left over, invest
that remaining money into an interest
bearing savings. Yet most Americans
are living from pay check to pay check,
having more bills at the end of the
month than money to pay.

The problem is that as long as we
continue to spend more than we have,
we can't start building wealth. Chronic

Wealth Builders: Michael McCain

overspending and high-interest, revolving credit card debt are your worst enemies when it comes to financial success. Spend like you're poor and you are much more likely to become rich. You don't have to spend every dime you have because you have it. Everyone likes new clothes, going out to eat and visiting events and places for enjoyment. Always remember to live within your means and save for the future while enjoying your current state of life.

Chapter Two:

The Power Of A Plan

Entrepreneurship runs all through my blood. I can remember talking with some business moguls and partners for hours planning new business ideas and the one thing I see that lacks consistently with neonate entrepreneurs is understanding "the power of a plan". Your business plan is like an introduction to the ins and outs of your business strategy. It's the number one thing that investors, future business partners, marketers, venture capitalist and banks will want to see to base a plan on their investment and potential loss that can come from the investment.

Reason #2: You don't have a plan.

I could remember a few years ago having a conference with a business partner and discussing all the types of business I wanted to start and how I was going to get there. I had ideas about everything I wanted to do but needed to put together a "life business plan" as to how I would get there and achieve those goals. I had an individual business plan for the business I was starting up but I now needed a "life business plan" that would pull my entire life into perspective with the goals and achievements I needed to make. It would be the blueprint that helps me build the foundation I needed and benchmark all the accomplishments I did achieve.

I would like to use what I have done as a partial example at building a life plan. Because I am a multitalented individual I could have picked from several different paths to take but which one would yield me the most rewards and benefits in the long run? I had to narrow it down to my love for writing and the number of books I had already written. Not only could I make a substantial income as a speaker and author but I now owned my own publishing company; building from a few books into a publishing brand known as Maximize Publishing Inc. From here I build the foundation to do some of the other things I've always dreamed and desired to do. Life Coaching, Public Speaking, Writing Novels and Turning them into movies and taking some of my life events and making documentaries; herein are a few examples of what I am able to do with writing out a life plan. This includes how much money I would like to make, invest, financial goals to reach with my books and etc.

Every person needs to take a moment and create a "Life Plan". Take a moment to write out what you desire to go to school for and why. What you desire to make as monthly income and how do you plan to get there. Where do you plan to work? What company will you work for? Will you start your own business? There are a plethora of questions that need to be pondered and answered when writing your life plan. I call it a life plan, others might call it a life business plan, and both are the self-same thing. When you have a life plan in place it give you something to run with, something to work towards building and achieving in life.

Without clearly defined short, mid and long-term goals, becoming rich will just seem like an unattainable fantasy; that turns into your go-to excuse for why you shouldn't bother saving or stop overspending. When you have clear cut goals and things to accomplish you know that every move you make and dollar you spends effects your long term and short term goals. You will be less likely to run your credit up or overspend not keeping in mind your financial needs and goals. As they say in the financial industry: those who fail to plan, plan to fail. Creating a financial plan may seem overwhelming or intimidating, but it doesn't have to be. Whether you do-it-yourself or decide to work with a financial professional, the process simply starts with prioritizing your goals and writing them down. Put that list where you can see it on a regular basis. Visual reminders go a long way in helping us stay on track. So the two key elements you need are:

1. A Life Plan
2. A Financial Plan

   With these two components you will be able to set in motion a plan for achieving your financial goals. Achieving the success you set out for in life. Climbing the ladder to staircase to wealth; you can hire a professional to help you put this together or use a basic business plan format to help you put everything in order. Make sure you include you current financial income, how much you can save, your regular spending obligations and how you plan to increase you income. Notice, the goal is to increase your income and not you're spending.

Wealth Builders: Michael McCain

Chapter Three:

Preparing For The Unexpected

One of the best ways to safeguard against unexpected emergencies is to create a budget to put money away for emergencies. It's no secret that things have a tendency of popping up when you least expect them. People who plan ahead always win because they count up the cost and prepare for unforeseen financial problems before they even have the opportunity to present themselves.

Reason #3: You don't have an emergency fund.

Wealth Builders: Michael McCain

I know you've heard it a hundred times: that you need to create an emergency fund. Yet, not many people paid attention to the value of this until the need arises and it's too late. Those needs could be such things as family or personal medical expenses, losing a job, unexpected home or car repair can take a toll on your income. These are expenses unprepared for. With an emergency fund you can offset some of these expenses that pop up and provide yourself with cushion to bounce back.

You need to have at least six months to a year's worth of income saved in an emergency fund. And yes, it's much easier said than done. However, I've seen too many people (including myself) get hit with a major unplanned expense, whether it's a car or home repair or a medical bill, or an unexpected job loss, accident or illness that's led to a drastic reduction in income. When these things happen–and they do, more often than you might think–not having a financial safety cushion can make the situation much, much worse. If you're forced to rely on credit cards, you'll end up sinking deeper into debt instead of, yes, saving to become rich.

In American culture we have trained ourselves to depend on student loans and income taxes as sources of income to help pay off bills, offset unexpected debts. These are the times we make changes, such as move, buy a new car, refurnish a home or make repairs on a home. This may not always be the best way of getting ahead. If you're receiving anything from 5,000 to 10,000 in tax returns you can put that money away into an interest bearing CD. Within a few years you can build an emergency fund and leave that money to grow and after 5 years have a total of 55,000 or more saved depending your interest rate or amount put into your savings fund.

I know some will want to argue that CD's may not offer the interest rates you would like to receive. There are online banks that offer higher interest rates than most traditional banks and you will have the opportunity to build your finances quicker than you would with the rates offered from traditional banks. It may accumulate money a little slower but in the long run when you have saved your initial balance and continue to flip it or leave it within your account to continue to draw interest you will have saved more money in a short time frame then you would by pinching pennies. If you want access to your money you can still but your money in an interest check or savings account. You may not get as much as you would with a CD but your money saved will be working for you. The goal is not to touch it but to save for emergency purposes.

Chapter Four:

So You Started Late?

For most of us that has been given the advantage of good parenting early in life were taught some basic skills for survival. Many of us had to learn responsibility either by our parents teaching us how to do things adults do to take care of themselves or you learned them out of necessity when no one else was there to care and provide. Either way you learn and develop the skills that are necessary for survival and life management. One of the easiest task most parent use is teaching their kids responsibility through there allowance. Teaching the responsibility of how to save and spend money. Usually this trickles over into adulthood and you learn both the value of hard work, paying bills and saving money.

Reason #4: You started late.

With every year or month that goes by without saving, your chances of becoming rich decrease. The earlier you start at learning to save and put away money the better your chances are at improving your financial outcome in life. Time and compounding interest are your two best friends when it comes to growing money, so wasting them really hurts. Just like exercising, the hardest part of saving is starting. Even if you're in debt, making little money or have a lot of expenses, you can still always save something — even if it is a small amount. The sooner you get yourself into the habit of saving — regardless of how much — the easier it will be for you to continue and eventually increase those savings. I like to think of saving as a muscle you have to work out and build with practice. Even if you start saving

Wealth Builders: Michael McCain

late, you can still become rich if you're committed enough. But you need to start. Now!!!

Look at it this way, if you save 100 dollars a month. By the end of the year you have 1,200 dollars. The following year you can put that money into a savings account or interest bearing CD that will allow that money to grow. If you continue this process year after year you will have saved a few thousand and made a few thousand off of your interest. Each year you may want to look into upgrading the amount you save. Next year you might want to save 200 and so on as time goes on.

As previously suggested you can use your income tax saving a few thousand or the sum total of your return to start an emergency fund or savings. Year after year saving half if not all will help you get ahead quicker and not have to work so hard at saving. Some other money making ideas would be to offer your talent, skills, services or expertise as a way to help you build money. If you are working a regular job but can babysit on

Wealth Builders: Michael McCain

weekends, tutor, walk dogs, edit papers, build websites, sing or cook for events it would be a great way to supplement your income and take what you make and save it.

Chapter Five:

All Talk & No Action

There are so many people that hold on to what I like to call "a story". These are the people who complain, make excuses for why they are in a terrible financial situation and why their financial plight is not improving yet they are all talk and take no action as to how they are going to improve their finances or quality of life. If there is going to be any change in your life you have to get up and take it by force. No one will have sympathy for your plight, the may show some concern for a while but no one will come along to lift a finger to help. You're an adult, you have to wear you big boy draws or your big girl panties and do what is needed to assure you success.

Wealth Builders: Michael McCain

Your education, criminal record and various excuses people use are not always sufficient to hold on to "a story" as to why you're not successful.

Reason #5: You'd rather complain than commit to action.

As the saying goes "there's nothing worse than a fool and his money". It's no secret that we all need to make wiser decisions with investing money. Many of us don't like to save money and often make poor decisions with spending. Then there are the complainers that spend and cry later that they did it because "it's not enough money to pay the bills I have" or "I am always short anyway I may as well enjoy the little I have". People who operate with this mindset usually have unpaid bills, mountains of debt in their names and more bills than there is money to pay them. People who operate with this mindset become emotionally irresponsible and usually will do careless spending to numb the pain. Making themselves feel better, providing a temporary fix when the real problem has not gone away at all. They complain day to day and continue providing excuses for their debt, behavior and current state of living.

"Life is too expensive." "I'll never get out of debt." "I don't make enough money." "Investing is too risky." I've probably heard every excuse for why someone isn't saving, investing or planning in general, and I'll admit I've used a few of them myself from time to time. There are times I have to shake myself and rid myself of adapting to these mindsets. I have to take a mental break and refocus on what my true plan and goal in life is and re-approach it with new vigor and energy. It's easier to be lazy and let bad habits fester than to commit to –and follow through on — changing them. It's no wonder obesity and debt are epidemics in our country, and that millions of Americans have had to push off retirement. People are getting older retiring broke and have to reenter the work force to provide what little income they can to survive.

The number one thing I would like every person reading this book to understand is your mindset about money has to change. Use this book as more than just a motivational tool to excite you about getting a plan for your life and a plan for your money. Take time to invest in your mind and educate yourself on new ways of making money as well as new ways of investing. Take time to educate yourself about the process before jumping into new business deals that may not end up paying off. Hire a debt counselor or professional accountant that can help you get your finances whipped into shape, someone who can help you improve your credit score, fico score and credit history.

Mind you, the goal for improving your credit should not be to burn up credit cards and put yourself in debt, but to earn a better status of living. How about investing in property and something that can increase in value, these should be the goals you have in mind for improving your credit and redeeming your name from creditors. As long as the complaining, excuses and finger-pointing persist, so too will not becoming rich. Instead, take responsibility for your bad habits and focus on what you can do to change them. Then do it.

Wealth Builders: Michael McCain

Chapter Six:

Living In The Moment

We all know someone who is caught up at "living in the moment". You may even be guilty of it yourself. I can remember in my younger years my father gave me a substantial amount of money to go to college and he was banking that I would be the one out of all his children to complete school and go straight to college. Well, I didn't do what my father wanted me to do. I attempted to go to college and dropped out. Needless to say I also carelessly spent the money that should have been for my education possibly with plenty to spare after.

Wealth Builders: Michael McCain

I have to say it was one of the more careless mistakes I made not knowing better at all. I was living for the moment. I was lavishing my then fiancé with clothes and gifts, taking my friends out to eat and going on trips all at my expense. I promise you I am not going to languish in the past but I want to make the point clear as to how easy it is to get caught up in the moment and not once think or plan for the future.

If I had place some thought to it I would have save money and invested in real estate or started a thriving business. It's funny how after you make all the careless mistakes you have plenty of time to sit and think about what you could have done differently and how you would have done it. Can you relate?

Reason #6: You live for today in spite of tomorrow.

I get it. It is really hard to think about retirement and other distant fantasies when we have needs and plenty of wants now. Depending your age and what stage you are at in life you may feel that you have plenty of time to worry about these things at some other point in your life. In your day to day life your more concerned with the bills have to get paid, the family must be fed; momma needs a vacation , Spending quality time with a significant other— finding a new wardrobe to go along with the trends and changes people are making. The problem is that impulsive and overly-indulgent behavior commonly leads to credit card debt and delinquencies on your credit report due to unpaid or mismanaged bills. Not to mention spending money you might have otherwise saved and, yes, not becoming rich!

Do yourself a favor: Ditch the "buy now, worry later" mindset and instead, adopt a "save now, get rich later" mindset. Learning to save money is imperative to your future for at least three main reasons that are outlined all throughout this book.

1. Education

2. Emergency Fund
3. Retirement

If you're going to be a wealth builder you have to implement financial management skills that encompass a broad scope of things.

1. Your current financial obligations
2. Your future financial plans
3. Your wealth building "blue print" or "life business plan"

If you are a compulsive shopper or believe in hobbies or spending that brings some form of pleasure to you or "therapy", these are dangerous habits to develop that will raise your risk level for creating or forming debt. It will also put you in a place of not having sufficient finances to be able to pay bill on time when they are due.

If you have no wealth being passed down to you from a family member your best bet is to build your blue print. It doesn't matter if you start early or late you can still grow your finances to a suitable place to add more comfort and stability to your everyday living. Of course the younger you are when you start the greater your chances. Some people fall prey to careless spending and living conditions because some dream or ideal life they wanted to live may not have come to pass for them. Some people struggle with age and give up thinking some things are impossible and therefore feel like they should lavish themselves because they may never get the dream life they have once targeted.

Realistically a general way of assessing the problems would be knowing if your goals and aspirations are realistic. Weeding out undetailed dreams or extremely lavish imagined lives may be the first step to correcting the issue and getting to the core reality of whether or not your dream is attainable.

Wealth Builders: Michael McCain

Chapter Seven:

Having All of Your Eggs In One
Basket

The worst thing anyone can do for
themselves is carelessly make
investments that bring no return.
Running after a particular stock,
investing in investment pools without
knowing all the details as to how the
benefit you or operate. You need to
know the risk factor and what can be
lost if your investment strategy does not

work out. This is why when it comes to investing your best bet is never to invest without a professional advisor or lawyer helping you to understand the process and the risk that can occur.

Reason #7: You're a one-trick investor.

You might be lucky enough to become rich by betting all your money on one type of investment. Investments are a type of gamble and will not always promise the types of returns that people expect. So if you make wealth by investing, you have stuck some luck and possibly some wise financial advisors. Then there are those that just might be lucky enough to win the lottery. But that's not a strategy for getting rich (at least, not one I'd ever recommend).

One of the worst financial mistakes you can make is putting all your money eggs in one basket. This is why making sure you get a financial advisor that can guide you through the ins and outs of investing would be wise. Putting all your eggs in one basket is not wise, spreading your money into well thought out investment strategies would give you the best results. Having all your eggs in one basket puts you at too much risk, whether it is being too conservative or too aggressive. Sure, the stock market is on a run and real estate is on an upswing again, but are you prepared for when the tides turn? Because they will, and if you are invested in all fixed-income securities like CDs, bonds and annuities and think you're safe, inflation should make you think again. Your investment portfolio needs to include a good mix of investments with varied levels of risk and return potential and liquidity (so you can get your money when you need it).

The poor and middle class aim for investing in CDS only. It's the only form of making money that they know or makes sense. Not too many poor families or middle class families have enough financial education to help guide how they invest. Having a diverse investment portfolio can help you grow your money quicker. There are secure ways to grow your money as well as some unsecure investments that you can make. The common mistake people make with investing is looking at the figures of what they speculate a return could be and becoming overzealous about their investments not knowing that stocks rise and fall on a day to day basis and a stock could be good today but fall tomorrow. Finding investment pools that grow slow and at a steady pace are better investment strategies that will help you win.

Chapter Eight:

I Would Save But I Spend Too Much

A person that is not willing to save and that's not willing to cut back on unnecessary spending is really not serious at all about getting out of debt and creating or building real wealth. If we take the time to consider all of the things we don't like about living in poverty and lack, it should remind us and give us the motivation necessary to stay motivated and committed to our goals and financial dreams.

Wealth Builders: Michael McCain

How many people hold on to excuses about all the luxuries we take for granted. Something's that we spend money on are completely unnecessary, you could live or make do without it but you just choose not to. While this chapter maybe short I want to provide and easy strategy that can be used to save money and make investments.

Reason #8: You don't automate.

I want to let you in on a secret most people don't practice when it comes to money. Here's the secret to saving: Automation. Saving is seamless when it's automatic. Unfortunately, we are not born to be savers. We are impulsive and greedy by nature. Being responsible requires much more discipline. However, automation forces us to be responsible without too much effort. And all it requires is setting up regular transfers from a paycheck or bank account to a savings or investment account. Banks allow you to do bill-pay where you can transfer set amounts of money on a monthly or biweekly basis. This is how some people pay their bills so they assure it's done on time and you can set up a savings or investment account the same way where you can have automatic transfers done for you where you may not have to be hands-on with making the effort to save or dealing with the temptation to spend.

Automation is a key strategy that can help you to save. Without it, we are much more likely to spend money we could be saving. Even if it is a seemingly small amount that you automate, those steady investments can make a big difference over time. Automate whatever you can whenever you can; just be careful to avoid over drafting your account and try to increase your savings amount periodically.

There are some old fashioned strategies that people use that sometimes don't work out well because people have a tendency to spend the money the save hidden in their homes tucked under the mattress, in a savings box or jar. When you know it's there you mind can't stay off of it and the temptation will present itself for you to dip in it or spend.

Only a disciplined person can save money from a secret jar, under a mattress or savings box and later put it towards a savings account, investments in stocks, bonds etc. This will only work if your faithful to taking your loose change as in coins or dollar bills from breaking a big bill and putting them away into a jar or box where when it is full you will find a CD, stock or bond to invest it in. You may use it to pay off some bills and clean up your credit, it's your money and the choice is yours. It's important to develop the habit to save money out of ever check your receive even down to loose change in a jar for unexpected moments that you can later turn over for bills and investing.

Chapter Nine:

Putting Today Off For Tomorrow

If you are serious about building wealth then you need a plan of action today! You can put today off for a year from now or when you pay off your loans, student loans and debt because if that remain the case you will never do it. You will never start on saving and building for the future. Some people refuse to allow their jobs to take out for retirement because they are worried about a few hundred dollars coming out of their check every two weeks. If that few hundred won't leave you broke and penniless at the end of each pay period it's a worthwhile investment that will help you secure your future.

The bottom line is you can put off today for tomorrow. You have to start making right choices today. If you are unaware as to how to go about planning for your financial future by all means hire an expert that can help you repair your credit and build your finances to the place they need to be. Waiting is simply wasting precious time and money.

Reason #9: You have no sense of urgency.

You might think you don't need to worry about getting out of debt or saving because someone or something else will save you. Maybe it's a pay raise, a new job, an inheritance, a rich spouse, or the lottery you're counting on.

Wealth Builders: Michael McCain

Whatever "it" is, you use it as an excuse to put off taking steps on your own to become rich. You need to rid yourself of all of this unrealistic ideas and pipe dreams that may never happen. The problem is that very little in life is certain. Who knows what will actually happen, or not happen, so why not focus on what you can control now? Save now and save yourself — just in case something, or someone, else won't.

You have to have urgency backing up your motives. If you never feel compelled to improve or make changes in your life you won't. If you don't feel compelled to change the way you spend money or save it, you really wont. Your best bet is to sit down and think about your vision for life realistically and how do you plan to create the dream life or a more improved life from the current state of your living. Set goals and set realistic stepping stones that will help you pave the way to getting there.

One of the examples of urgency was being slapped with the reality of my son being born. While I was at the time married, we were young and enjoying life not giving any thought to the future on how to even prepare for family. One of the sense of urgency that was created for me was that I now had another mouth to feed and I had to prepare for all the things my son would need and emergencies that will arise. At this time of my life I was operating a cleaning business that was doing very well. I had more money that I knew how to spend yet I never saved or invested like I should have.

What it all boils down to is that panic feeling you get when your life changes or some type of emergency occurs that brings you into reality of the changes that need to be made in your life. Usually when this happens it shows you how unprepared you are or the carelessness that you have been living under. Sometimes these occurrences turn out to be the perfect wakeup call and opportunity for change and with the right steps in place you can make a significant turnaround putting your life on tract.

Wealth Builders: Michael McCain

What I want every reader to walk away with today is the urgency to begin to save money, learn how and where to invest and building a greater financial education. Your financial education is key in helping you both to sustain and grow the wealth that you are trying to build. The lottery and get rich quick schemes will not payoff it will be a waste of time, energy and not to mention MONEY!

Wealth Builders: Michael McCain

Chapter Ten:

The Power of Influence

I opened this book by talking about the power of influence that the media has and there are other forms of influence that exist in our lives such as trends with hobbies, fashion and games. There also the influence of family, spouses and friends that can make an impact on the way we choose to spend our money.

Wealth Builders: Michael McCain

The matter of importance at hand is assessing what influences you to spend and harnessing the power as to how you can create change.

Reason #10: You're easily influenced.

Maybe you live with a chronic over spender or a typical day out with your girlfriends or friends involves shopping. Or maybe it's your inner "Real Housewife" that you sometimes can't control. Or how about the boredom that you feel or sometimes loneliness that contributes to emotional spending; most people call it "retail therapy" when they take a little time to spend and by things that make them feel better. We all have negative influences in our lives that threaten our chances of becoming rich. The superficial, materialistic, sensational culture in which we live is probably the biggest one. People feel enticed by the wealth of celebrities and fall prey to the latest trends and fads trying to keep up.

Wealth Builders: Michael McCain

The suffocating swirl of media that goes along with it makes it ten times worse. Not everything that we see portrayed over television is absolute truth. Think about all the "get rich quick" programs we have seen all over T.V. promising to "Unlock the secrets of the rich". Everyone finds themselves buying into it and still end up broke. Some of the simplistic ways to build wealth are the very things everyday people don't want to do or believe. Playing the lotto is another poor get rich tactic people use with the odds and chances of winning one to possible millions who have played into the same game. Some old fashioned ways of getting to wealth would be getting a good education to work at a well-paying job while learning to save and invest. The younger you are when you begin saving increases your chances for wealth later in life if you follow and improve on that pattern as you grow.

The trick is not giving in to temptation. How? Some of it is making conscious choices to avoid putting yourself in vulnerable positions. But most of it is having the willpower to keep the goal of becoming rich in the front of your mind, especially when you are tempted to sabotage yourself. You have to ditch all those compulsive behaviors and implement behaviors that bring you wealth and security.

Other Books by the Author:

1. **The Purpose Driven Prayer Life**

2. **Prayerology** T.M.- **The School Of Prayer**

3. **Soul Cleanse Vol. I**

4. **Epiphany Letters**

5. **The Newborn Entrepreneur**

6. The Millionaire Class Vol. 1

7. The Recession Millionaire

8. Recession Lessons T.M.

Personal Memoirs by the author:

9. My Quarter Life Experience

10. Diary of an Ex-Husband

All the above mentioned books
published with Maximize Publishing
Inc. Bronx New York.

About The Author

Dr. Michael McCain, best known as a motivational speaker, author. Yet there's more to his experience and story Dr. McCain is also a poet, entrepreneur, life coach and spiritual teacher. Michael has a wide range of experience both in business and in the non-profit religious sector.

Best known as the General in the Art of Strategic Prayer and Spiritual Warfare, The Author of "Prayerology" Michael McCain is a life coach, Prophetic voice and Ambassador of Hope. Dr. Michael McCain is a 21st Century World Leader who has partnered with business moguls, politicians and church, civic world leaders for more than 15 years to equip and empower millions to maximize their potential.

As one of the leading voices of our time, he founded Dr. Michael McCain Enterprises Inc. (DMME), Kaleo University, as well as a conglomerate of companies and business to bring practical solutions to spiritual and social ills; effecting change within our communities while transforming the course of our global destiny. His track record as a revolutionary thinker and prolific communicator, has established him as one of the most respected and sought-after youthful leaders in the world today.

Wealth Builders: Michael McCain

Wealth Builders: Michael McCain